Can You Count In Greek?
Exploring Ancient Number Systems

Written by **Judy Leimbach** and **Kathy Leimbach**
Illustrated by **Dean Crawford**

 Routledge
Taylor & Francis Group

NEW YORK AND LONDON

First published in 2005 by Prufrock Press Inc.

Published 2021 by Routledge
605 Third Avenue, New York, NY 10017
2 Park Square, Milton Park, Abingdon, Oxon OX14 4RN

Routledge is an imprint of the Taylor & Francis Group, an informa business

ISBN 13: 978-1-5936-3056-0 (pbk)

Contents

Introduction

Development of Number Systems

For thousands of years people existed without the need for numbers or number symbols. They were wanderers and gatherers and their only concept of numbers was limited to the concepts of *greater than* and *less than*. As people began to develop agriculture and raise animals, they needed to keep track of their possessions. At first they counted on their fingers or made simple tally marks. In time, however, as they began to trade and lived in larger groups, they needed more formalized number systems to keep track of their transactions. They gradually developed symbols for numbers and then systems of numeration that included rules for using these symbols. Several different systems were developed by various cultures. Ideas were borrowed from other civilizations and adapted to local resources and symbols. The earliest systems had only a few symbols and used the repetition of those symbols to denote larger numbers. Later systems used more symbols and developed more sophisticated systems for using the symbols to denote numbers. Some of these systems are still in use today, but many of the early systems have been discarded because they were not convenient for representing larger numbers or for use with computing.

Why Study Other Number Systems?

Can You Count in Greek? introduces students to some of these early number systems. Studying these other number systems and their underlying principles leads students to a greater understanding and appreciation of our own number system. The units in this book present some of the history of numerals and systems of numeration. They develop an understanding of the concepts of numerals as number symbols, as well as the principles that were used in conjunction with these symbols.

When discussing the origin of the concept of number with your students consider notions of "more than," "less than" and "equal" as concepts coming before any written system. Perhaps fingers or sticks or stones were first used to represent numbers. The tally system was probably developed as civilization developed a need to be able to answer the question "how many?" Once students have used these earlier, cumbersome number systems, they will appreciate the efficiency of the decimal system.

About This Book

Teacher's Section – The information in the teacher's section is meant to be a brief overview for the instructor on the various numeration systems included in the book. Further understanding of each system can be gained by working through the student pages.

Student's Pages – Each unit begins with a brief history of the civilization that developed the system. The symbols and rules regarding the use of the symbols to represent numbers are then introduced and demonstrated with examples. Each page also provides problems that let students apply their understandings. An extension page or a comparison page at the end of each unit has been included to further challenge advanced math students.

Instructor's Explanation of the Number Systems

Egyptian Number System

The Egyptian hieroglyphic system dates back as early as 3000 B.C. and was in use for about two thousand years. It was an additive system using the repetitive principle. A symbol was repeated to represent the numbers between its value and the value of the next symbol. To determine the value of a numeral, the values of all the symbols were added. In an additive system like this, with no place value, the order in which the symbols appeared did not matter.

The Egyptian hieroglyphic system used the following notation.

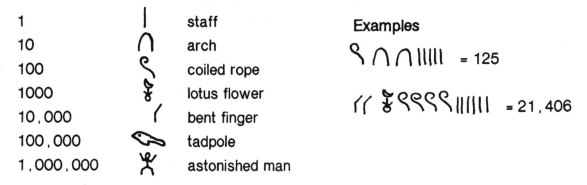

1		staff	**Examples**
10		arch	
100		coiled rope	∫ ∩ ∩ ||||| = 125
1000		lotus flower	
10,000		bent finger	ↄↄ ⚇ ℛℛℛℛ ||||| = 21,406
100,000		tadpole	
1,000,000		astonished man	

The Egyptian system is easy to learn and understand. Practice in interpreting this system reinforces understanding of our own decimal system. Writing numbers in this system develops appreciation for the efficiency of our system.

The Babylonian System

The Babylonian numeration system was developed more than 5000 years ago in the part of the world that is now Iraq. This ancient civilization was named for the city of Babylon, which no longer exists. The Babylonians did not have papyrus or other paper-like materials to write on. They wrote with a wedge-shaped stylus on clay tables. This type of writing is called "cuneiform" writing, which means "wedge-shaped" in Latin.

The Babylonian system was like other ancient systems in that it started with tally marks. Wedges pointing down represented the numbers from 1 to 9.

| = 1 ||| = 3 |||/|| = 5 |||/|||/| = 7 |||/|||/||| = 9

Multiples of 10 from 10 to 50 were represented by wedges pointing left.

◄ = 10   ◄◄ = 20   ◄◄◄/◄◄ = 50

Numbers less than sixty were written by combining the symbols for ten and one. The tens were placed to the left of the ones.

< III
< I = 24

<<< III
<< II = 55

<< I
<< = 41

The Babylonian system was based on **sixty** and did have place value. Wedges placed to the left of the tens, represented **sixties**. Wedges placed to the left of the tens and the sixties represented **sixty sixties** or 3,600. In this book, we do not deal with numerals larger than 3,599, but if you have students who easily grasp the place-value system of the Babylonians, you may wish to extend their practice to include larger numbers.

I **< II** = 82
(1x60) + (2x10) + (2x1)

III
II **<< I** = 331
(5x60) + (3x10) + (1x1)

< III
< II <<< III = 1,543
(25x60) + 43

<< << < III
II **< III I<< < I** = 9,224
(2x3600) + (33x60) + 44

The Babylonians had no symbol for zero. They simply left a blank space within the numeral they were writing to indicate that there were no ones, tens, sixties, etc. This could be very confusing. Sometimes they used a dot to separate wedges pointing the same direction. They never really thought of the dot as we think of zero. They used it only as a **divider**, not as a place holder.

I I · I = 121
(120) + (0x10) + (1)

III
II · II = 302
(300) + (0x10) + (2)

The Greek System

The ancient Greeks' number system was an additive system consisting of twenty-seven symbols, the twenty-four letters of the Greek alphabet plus three additional symbols for the obsolete digamma, koppa, and sampi. The symbols and their values were:

A	alpha	1	I	iota	10	P	rho	100
B	beta	2	K	kappa	20	Σ	sigma	200
Γ	gamma	3	Λ	lambda	30	T	tau	300
Δ	delta	4	M	mu	40	Υ	upsilon	400
E	epsilon	5	N	nu	50	Φ	phi	500
	obsolete digamma	6	Ξ	xi	60	X	chi	600
Z	zeta	7	O	omicron	70	Ψ	psi	700
H	eta	8	Π	pi	80	Ω	omega	800
Θ	theta	9		obsolete koppa	90		obsolete sampi	900

Numerals were written by combining the symbols and adding their values.

$$XOA = 671 \qquad M\Delta = 44 \qquad P\Xi\Gamma = 163 \qquad KH = 28$$

To write multiples of 1000 the Greeks used the first nine symbols along with a prime symbol (').

$$A' = 1,000 \qquad Z' = 7,000 \qquad \Gamma'TN = 3,350$$

To write multiples of 10,000 they used the first nine symbols grouped with a M. Some references show the M written to the right of the unit symbol (BM = 2x10,000 = 20,000) and some references show the unit symbol written on top of the M. We have chosen to use the notation that shows the M written under the unit symbol. In either case, the combination meant that the value for the unit symbol was multiplied by 10,000.

$$\underset{M}{A} = 10,000 \qquad \underset{M}{Z} = 70,000 \qquad \underset{M}{B} = 20,000$$

83,400 was written $M\overset{H}{\Gamma}'\Upsilon$ and 72,452 was $M\overset{Z}{B}'\Upsilon NB$.

The main disadvantage to the Greek system was that it necessitated memorizing so many different symbols. Obviously, students should not be required to memorize these symbols, but should be allowed to refer to the chart. Another disadvantage was the confusion that could be created by having the same symbol represent a letter as well as a number. The main advantage the Greek system had over other ancient systems was that large numbers could be written using far fewer symbols.

7

The Roman System ━━

This numeration system, which is still in use to a limited extent today, dates back to the ancient Romans. It is primarily an additive system using letters as symbols. The symbols and their values are:

I = 1	L = 50	M = 1,000
V = 5	C = 100	
X = 10	D = 500	

Numerals are written by repetition of these symbols (written from largest to smallest).

XXXVII = 37   CCLXXIII = 273   MMCCCXXXI = 2,331

The system also involves the **subtractive** principle. If a symbol of a smaller number comes before the symbol of a larger number, the two are considered as a pair and the smaller number is subtracted from the larger.

IV = 4   XL = 40   IX = 9   XC = 90

The subtractive principle is restricted to the numerals for four and nine, forty and ninety, four hundred and nine hundred. The student page for "Rules for Writing Roman Numerals" explains the rules regarding this principle in detail. Note that use of the subtractive principle makes **ordering** of the symbols important.

The largest number that can be written using the seven letters is MMMCMXCIX (3,999). For larger numerals, multiples of 1,000 are indicated by writing a bar above the symbol.

$\overline{X}$ = 10,000 $\overline{XL}$ = 40,000 $\overline{IV}$CCX = 4,210

Likewise, a double bar means multiplying the symbol by 1,000,000.

$\overline{\overline{X}}$ = 10,000,000 $\overline{\overline{XL}}$ = 40,000,000 $\overline{\overline{IV}}$CCX = 4,000,210

Hindu–Arabic System ━━━━━━━━━━━━━━━━━━━━━━━━━━━━━━━━━━━━━━

This number system, which we use today, was developed in India by the Hindus. It was introduced to the Western world by the Arabs. About 2,000 years ago the Hindu numbers looked different (though similar) from the symbols we use today. Over time the symbols changed and with the invention of the printing press became standardized.

Later in the 5th century, the Hindus developed the idea of zero. This made possible the place value system we use today. Before that they had special symbols for 10, 20, 30, 40, 50, 60, 70, 80, 90, 100 and 1,000. To write a number like 3,465 they would write the symbol for 3 and the symbol for 1000, then the symbol for 4 and the symbol for 100, then the symbol for 60 and the symbol for 5.

Instructor's Explanation, continued

The invention of zero and the development of place value is what made the Hindu-Arabic system better than other systems. The main advantages are economy of symbols and adaptability to computation. These advantages made this a system of numeration that gained great popularity and survived the test of time.

The Hindu-Arabic system uses ten symbols and is a place value system based on powers of ten. This means the first place on the right represents ones and each place to the left represents ten times the place on its right. Today it is called the decimal system because it is based on the number 10. After studying other place value systems, students should find this familiar system easy to understand and use. An example of decimal notation is the following.

$$673 = (6 \times 100) + (7 \times 10) + (3 \times 1) \qquad 4,782 = (4 \times 1000) + (7 \times 100) + (8 \times 10) + (2 \times 1)$$

Quinary System

The quinary number system is like the decimal system, except that it is based on **five** rather than ten. It uses five numerals 0, 1, 2, 3, and 4. Since its place value system is based on five, the first place on the right represents ones and each place to the left represents five times the place to its right. A place value chart and an example of numerals in this system would look like the following.

(5×125)	(5×25)	(5×5)	(5×1)	(1)
625	125	25	5	1

$$123 = (1 \times 25) + (2 \times 5) + (3 \times 1) = 38_{10} \qquad 1402 = (1 \times 125) + (4 \times 25) + (0 \times 5) + (2 \times 1) = 227_{10}$$

Counting in this system would look like this.

1, 2, 3, 4, 10, 11, 12, 13, 14, 20, 21, 22, 23, 24, 30, 31, 32, 33, 34, 40, 41, 42, 43, 44, 100, 101, 102, 103, 104, 110, etc.

"10" must be read "one-zero" (not ten) since it represents one five and no ones (or five). "100" must be read "one-zero-zero" (not one hundred) since it represents one twenty-five, no fives, and no ones (or 25).

When writing numbers in a system based on a number other than ten, we sometimes use a notation written smaller and to the lower right of the numeral to indicate what the base is. For example:

12_5	12 in base 5
200_3	200 in base 3
1011_2	1011 in base 2

Binary System

The binary system is based on the number two and uses only two numerals; 0 and 1. Since it is based on powers of two, the first place on the right is ones and each place to the left represents two times the place on its right. A place value chart and an example of a numeral written in the binary number system would look like this.

(2x64)	(2x32)	(2x16)	(2x8)	(2x4)	(2x2)	(2x1)	(1x1)
128	64	32	16	8	4	2	1

$101 = (1\times4) + (0\times2) + (1\times1) = 5_{10}$ $10110 = (1\times16) + (0\times8) + (1\times4) + (1\times2) + (0\times1) = 22_{10}$

The binary system is used by computers. Electronic switches that control the flow of electricity can be "on" or "off" as designated by 1 or 0.

The Mayan System

The Mayans lived in Central America from about 1500 B.C. to A.D. 1500. Without knowledge of any of the European or Asian number systems, they developed an interesting system using dots and bars. The remarkable thing about the Mayan system is that it had a symbol for zero and it had a place value.

The Mayan system was a base-twenty system. What seems very unusual to us was that their place value was vertical rather than horizontal. The Mayans used dots to represent the numerals from 1 to 4. They used a bar for 5. The numerals from 1 to 19 were written with a combination of bars and dots as shown below.

To write 20 they used one dot in the twenties' place (which was above the units' place) and a symbol for zero (thought to represent a clam shell) in the units' place. Numerals larger than 20 were designated by indicating multiples of 20 combined with units' values.

Instructor's Explanation, continued

In the Mayan system, the numeral for 45 looks very much like the numeral for 7. The difference is in the spacing. In the 7 the dots are close to the bar; in the 45 there is more space between the dots and the bar.

When the Mayans reached 360, they used a modified base 20 system. Instead of using 20x20 as the next place value, they used 18x20 (360). Likewise, the next place value was 18x20x20 (7,200) instead of 20^3. This inconsistency may be difficult for students to understand. If so, you may want to only present the first four lessons for this number system. The following, shows how to write larger Mayan numerals.

Primitive Number Symbols

We use symbols like **1, 2, 3** and **4** to represent numbers. These symbols have not always been used to represent numbers. For a long time, humans had no need to count or write down numbers. Then thousands of years ago people began to herd animals. When this happened, they needed some way to count the number of animals in their herds. This was probably done with pebbles, marks in the dirt or scratches on a rock. They probably had only one numeral, a mark that stood for the number one (I). To keep track of bigger numbers, they had to repeat that same mark or numeral for each thing they counted.

IIIIIII meant seven

IIIIIIIIIIIIIIIII meant seventeen

IIIIIIIIIIIIIIIIIIIIIIIIIII meant twenty–seven

One of the first great improvements in this early number system was probably separating the marks into groups of five. This was done by making the fifth mark cross the first four marks like ⊤⊬ .

What numbers are represented by the symbols below?

⊤⊬ ⊤⊬ ⊤⊬ ⊤⊬ ⊤⊬ I   _____

⊤⊬ ⊤⊬ ⊤⊬ ⊤⊬ ⊤⊬ ⊤⊬ III   _____

Why was grouping by fives a big improvement? _____

_____

What are the main disadvantages of this system?_____

_____

Egyptian Number System

The Egyptians lived in the fertile Nile Valley. As early as 5,000 years ago they developed a rich farming community that nourished prosperous cities, markets, trading connections, and a government. They needed a system of writing and computing in order to keep records for their commerce and government. They developed a system of writing called hieroglyphics, and they developed a number system in which there were picture symbols to represent the numbers one, ten, and powers of ten. They also learned how to make a kind of paper from the stems of papyrus plants that grew along the Nile river, so there were written records of their transactions.

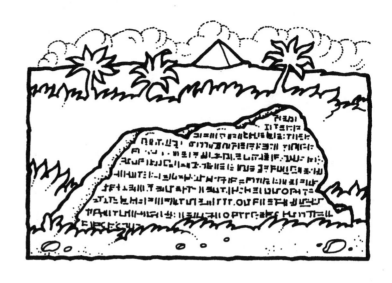

These are some of the picture symbols they used.

1	|	a staff
10	∩	an arch
100	୧	a coiled rope
1,000	⚘	a flower

This was a **big improvement** over the old tally system. They could write a number like 3,000 using only 3 symbols instead of 3,000 symbols the more primitive system required. To write a number like 1,423 the Egyptians used 10 symbols. They would write something that looked like this.

⚘ ୧୧୧୧ ∩∩ ||| = 1000 + 100 + 100 + 100 + 100 + 10 + 10 + 1 + 1 + 1

There was **no place value** in the Egyptian system. Symbols could be written in any order.

2,365 could be written   ⚘||| ୧୧⚘ ∩∩∩ ୧|| ∩∩∩

2,365 could also be written   ⚘⚘ ୧୧୧ ∩∩∩∩∩∩ |||||

How many symbols would it take to write the following?

47   _____   248   _____

672   _____   5,309   _____

Count Like an Egyptian

Interpret the Egyptian numerals below and write what they would equal in our number system.

1. |||∩∩∩∩૧ _____

2. ∩∩૧૧૧૧૧ _____

3. ||||||૧૧૧૧૧૧૬૬ _____

4. |∩∩∩∩૧૧૧૧૧૧૧ _____

5. |||||||∩∩∩ _____

6. ||∩૧૧૧૧૬૬૬ _____

7. ૧૧૧૧૧૧૬ _____

8. ||||||||||૧૧ _____

9. ||∩∩∩∩∩∩∩૧૧૧૧૧ _____

10. |||∩∩∩૧૬૬૬૬ _____

11. ||||||૧૧૧૬૬૬ _____

12. ∩∩∩∩∩૧૧૧૧૬ _____

13. ||∩∩∩∩∩∩૧૬૬૬૬૬ _____

14. ∩∩∩∩∩૬૬૬ _____

15. ૧૧૧૧૧||∩∩∩ _____

16. ||||૬૬૬૬∩∩ _____

17. |||||૬૬૧૧૧ _____

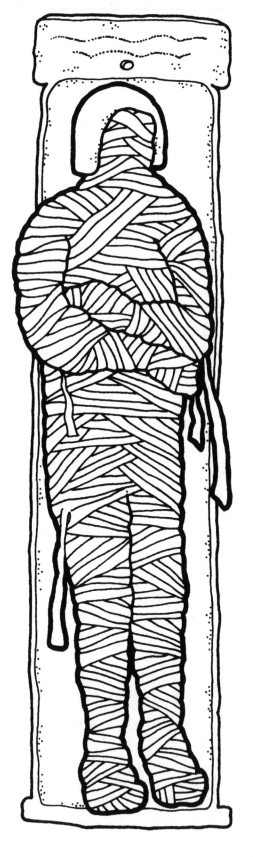

Write Like an Egyptian

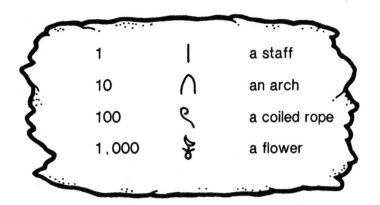

1	|	a staff
10	∩	an arch
100	ℓ	a coiled rope
1,000	⚘	a flower

Use Egyptian symbols to write these numbers.

1. 73 _____

2. 139 _____

3. 470 _____

4. 602 _____

5. 3,471_____

6. 1,094_____

7. 2,506_____

Use >, < or = to compare these numbers.

8. ‖∩∩ ◯ ‖‖‖‖‖‖‖∩∩

9. ‖‖‖‖∩∩∩∩∩∩∩ ◯ \|ℓ

10. ‖∩ℓℓℓ ◯ ℓℓℓ‖‖∩

11. ∩∩∩∩ℓℓℓ ◯ ‖‖‖‖∩∩ℓℓℓℓ

12. ‖\|ℓℓ⚘⚘ ◯ ‖∩∩⚘⚘

Larger Egyptian Numerals

When ancient Egyptians needed to write numerals larger than 9,999 they used different symbols than those for the first four numerals. These are the symbols they had for larger numbers.

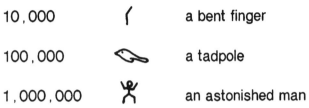

10,000	(	a bent finger
100,000	◁	a tadpole
1,000,000	☥	an astonished man

Use the Egyptian symbols above to write these numerals.

1. 50,000 _____

2. 600,000 _____

3. 2,000,000 _____

4. 320,000 _____

5. 250,000 _____

6. 1,400,000 _____

7. 1,070,000 _____

8. 2,200,000 _____

How many symbols would it take to write 57,832? _____

How many symbols would it take to write 999,999? _____

Even though it takes a lot of symbols to write these numerals, it is still much better than the primitive tally system. How many symbols would it have taken primitive people to write 999,999? _____

Egyptian Review

Translate the numerals below into our number system.

1. ‖∩∩∩ʕ⦚⦚   _____

2. ∩ʕʕʕ𐎚𐎚⦚⦚⁂   _____

3. ‖∩∩∩∩∩∩𐎚𐎚𐎚⦚⦚ꞵꞵ   _____

4. ‖‖ʕ𐎚𐎚⦚⦚⦚   _____

5. ‖‖‖‖∩∩∩∩𐎚𐎚𐎚𐎚 ꞵ   _____

6. ∩∩∩ʕʕʕ𐎚𐎚𐎚ꞵꞵꞵ⁂⁂   _____

7. ʕʕʕ⦚⦚⦚⦚⦚ ꞵꞵ   _____

8. ‖‖‖‖‖∩∩∩ʕ𐎚⦚⦚⦚⦚⦚⦚⦚   _____

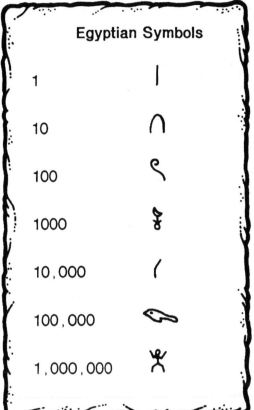

Egyptian Symbols	
1	ǀ
10	∩
100	ʕ
1000	𐎚
10,000	⦚
100,000	ꞵ
1,000,000	⁂

Write the following in the Egyptian number system.

9. 24,612   _____

10. 120,534   _____

11. 1,042,015   _____

12. 4,010,378   _____

13. 44,035   _____

14. 314,275   _____

Egyptian Computation

Egyptians could easily add and subtract numbers, but multiplication and division were much more complicated. Adding and subtracting using Egyptians numerals is basically like making change with money. Try adding and subtracting the numbers below. You may need to regroup.

Example:

1.	2.
3.	4.
5.	6.
7.	8.

Hint: You can check your work by converting the Egyptian numerals into our number system and doing the computations.

The Babylonian Number System

Thousands of years ago between the Tigris and Euphrates Rivers, in the part of the world that is now called Iraq, stood the ancient city of Babylon. The Babylonians were traders and merchants, so they needed math to keep track of their transactions. They did not have any paper-like materials like the Egyptians had. Instead, they wrote on clay tablets. They pressed a wedge-shaped instrument (called a stylus) into the clay while it was soft. Later the tablets were baked until they were hard. This type of writing was called **cuneiform** writing. This wedge-shaped writing on clay was used by many civilizations for about 3,000 years.

The Babylonians used only two kinds of wedge-shaped marks to write every number. The two symbols they used were

a wedge pointing down   **❙**   meaning *one*

and a wedge pointing left   **◀**   meaning *ten*.

The Babylonians wrote numerals from one to nine using the wedge that pointed downward. Notice how they grouped the wedges in threes for easier reading.

❙ = 1	❙❙❙ = 4	❙❙❙ ❙ = 7
❙❙ = 2	❙❙❙ ❙❙ = 5	❙❙❙ ❙❙❙ ❙❙ = 8
❙❙❙ = 3	❙❙❙ ❙❙❙ = 6	❙❙❙ ❙❙❙ ❙❙❙ = 9

To write tens they used the wedge pointing to the left. Multiples of ten were written as follows.

◀◀ = 20   ◀◀◀ = 30   ◀◀◀ ◀◀ = 50

Numbers less than sixty were written by combining the symbols for one and ten. The **tens** were placed to the **left** of the **ones**.

◀❙❙❙ = 13   ◀◀❙❙❙ ❙❙❙ = 26   ◀◀◀❙❙ = 32

◀◀❙❙❙ ◀◀❙ = 44   ◀◀❙❙❙ ◀◀❙❙❙ ❙ = 47   ◀◀❙❙❙ ◀◀❙❙❙ ◀❙❙❙ = 59

Reading and Writing Babylonian Numerals

Read the Babylonian numerals below and write what they equal in our number system.

1. <<< !!! !!! _____

2. <<< < !!! << !! _____

3. < < ! _____

4. << !!! << ! _____

5. <<< !!! _____

6. < !!! ! _____

7. << < !! _____

8. << !!! < !!! !!! _____

Write these numerals in the Babylonian system.

9. 19

10. 24

11. 38

12. 42

13. 51

14. 59

A Bright Babylonian Idea

The Babylonians came up with a completely new idea. They discovered the idea of place value. Place value means that the value of a symbol depends on its placement in the numeral. The Babylonian system was not a true place-value system, though, because they did not use a symbol for zero. In devising their system, they used a combination of both a base-ten and a base-sixty system. They used the simple system of vertical and horizontally-placed wedges until they reached 59. Then they switched to a base 60 system. A wedge pointing downward place to the left of the ten's position stood for sixty (60).

Their place value system looked like this.

60's	10's	1's

For example, the numeral 76 would be written as

This represented (1 x 60) + (1 x 10) + (6 x 1)

This sometimes made reading numerals confusing. It was hard to tell what a single symbol stood for. Sometimes they used a small dot as a divider or place holder. It meant that there were no tens or no sixties. It was never placed at the end of a numeral.

Here are a few examples.

60 + 15 = 75

60 + 5 = 65

120 + 3 = 123

180 + 16 = 196

300 + 50 + 9 = 359

420 + 4 = 424

What are these Babylonian numerals in our system?

a.

b.

c.

d.

e.

f.

Reading Larger Babylonian Numerals

Review the rules for writing numerals using the Babylonian number system. Then translate the Babylonian numerals below into our number system.

1. << ¦¦¦ << ¦	2. ¦¦ << ¦¦¦ <<

3. ¦¦¦ <	4. < ¦¦¦
	   ¦ < ¦¦¦
	     ¦¦¦

5. << ¦¦¦
    < ¦
	6. ¦¦¦ < ¦¦¦
	   ¦¦ < ¦¦¦
	     ¦¦¦

7. ¦¦¦ · ¦¦¦ ¦¦¦ · ¦¦¦	8. ¦¦ < ¦¦ <

9. ¦¦¦ · ¦¦¦
   ¦ · ¦¦¦
      ¦
	10. ¦¦¦ <<
	   ¦ << ¦¦¦

Babylonian Review

Write these as Babylonian numerals.

a. 47	b. 100
c. 446	d. 121
e. 575	f. 537

Translate these Babylonian numerals to our number system.

g. << III << III III	h. I << III I < III

i.   III << III
   II << III
    II II	

j. II · II	

Even Larger Babylonian Numerals

The largest numeral you have been able to write so far using the Babylonian system is 599 (9 sixties + 5 tens + 9 ones). To write larger numerals, you would indicate multiples of sixty just as you did with tens and ones. That is, once you have shown nine sixties, you would use wedges pointed to the left to indicate ten sixties. You will then have a grouping of wedges pointing down and to the left indicating the number of tens and ones and a grouping of wedges pointing down and to the left that indicate the number of sixties. Here are some examples.

$$(19 \times 60) + (5 \times 10) + (3 \times 1) = 1140 + 50 + 3 = 1,193$$

$$(22 \times 60) + (2 \times 10) + (5 \times 1) = 1320 + 20 + 5 = 1345$$

Read these Babylonian numerals.

a.	b.
c.	d.
e.	f.

Write these as Babylonian numerals.

g. 797	h. 234
i. 808	j. 1,000

© Taylor & Francis — *Can You Count In Greek?*

Roman Number System

About 3,000 years ago the Romans developed a number system that used **letters** as **numerals**. Around 250 B.C. Rome began to gain control of the whole Mediterranean, and in time the Romans conquered and ruled an empire that included most of southern Europe, France, Britain and parts of northern Africa. During the days of the mighty Roman Empire, the Roman civilization spread and their number system was used throughout much of Europe. We still use Roman numerals today.

The Romans used the following letter symbols for numerals. The numerals from 1 to 39 can be written using these three symbols.

I = 1   V = 5   X = 10

The Roman system of numeration was an additive system. This means that a numeral is the sum of the numbers represented by each symbol. They did not have place value. However, the **order** of the number symbols was important. These Roman numerals show how the repetitive use of the symbols was used to write numerals.

III = 3   VII = 7   XIII = 13   XVI = 16   XXXVII = 37

In all of the numerals above you should notice these things:
1. Symbols for the same numeral are grouped together.
2. Smaller numerals are placed to the right of larger numerals.
3. You add the value of the symbols to find the numeral represented.

The Subtraction Rule

The subtraction rule stated that when a smaller numeral was placed to the left of a larger numeral, the smaller numeral was subtracted from the larger numeral. This meant that a symbol would never be repeated more than three times in a numeral. For example, to write thirty-four you would write **XXXIV** (30 + 5 - 1) instead of XXXIIII. This principle was used only a little during ancient and medieval times but is used consistently in modern times. Here are some examples.

IV = 4   XIV = 14   IX = 9   XXIX = 29   XXXIV = 34

Write these Roman numerals in our number system.

a) VI =_____   b) IV =_____   c) XI = _____   d) IX=_____

e) XVI =_____   f) XXXIV =_____   g) XXXIII =_____   h) XIX =_____

More Roman Numerals

As we learned previously, the Romans used the following symbols for the numbers one, five, and ten.

I = 1   V = 5   X = 10

In addition to these symbols, they had other symbols to represent numbers larger than ten. These were:

L = 50   C = 100

The same rules that were used for smaller numerals applied to these larger numerals. Larger numerals were written like the following.

CLXXI = 171 (100 + 50 + 20 + 1)

CCCLXXXVII = 387 (300 + 50 + 30 + 5 + 2)

XLVII = 47 (50 - 10) + (5 + 2)   CCLXXIX = 279 (200 + 50 + 20 + 10 - 1)

Write the Roman numerals below in our number system. Remember to add the symbols, unless a symbol with a smaller value appears before a larger symbol (then you subtract it).

1. LXII _____

2. LXXV _____

3. LIX _____

4. XLVIII _____

5. CL _____

6. CLXXI _____

7. CLXIV _____

8. CXXXIX _____

9. CXLI _____

10. CIX _____

11. CVI _____

12. XLIX _____

13. XC _____

14. CCLV _____

15. CCCXXX _____

16. CLXXVII _____

17. CXLIV _____

18. CCXIX _____

19. CXCV _____

20. LXXXVIII _____

21. CCXLIII _____

22. CCCLXIV _____

23. CCXCVI _____

24. CCXLIV _____

Larger Roman Numerals

The largest numeral the Romans wrote using I, V, X, L and C was 399. To write larger numerals they needed more symbols. The other two symbols they used for writing larger numerals were **D** for **500** and **M** for **1000**. The same rules applied for these larger numerals. That is, symbols were added to get the value of the numeral. If a symbol with a smaller value appeared before one with a larger value, it was subtracted. These symbols were used in the following ways to represent larger numerals.

DC = 600	CD = 400	DCC = 700
DCCC = 800	CM = 900	MDCC = 1700

Write the following Roman numerals in our number system.

1. DC _____

2. MD _____

3. DCCXL _____

4. MCCXXIV _____

5. CDXXXIX _____

6. MMCCCX _____

7. CMLXXV _____

8. MCDXII _____

9. CMXLIV _____

10. MCM _____

11. MCDXCII _____

12. DCLV _____

13. MDCCC _____

14. DCCCX _____

15. MDLV _____

16. MCDV _____

17. MMMXL _____

18. CDXL _____

19. MDCCLXXVI _____

20. MMMDCIX _____

21. MMCMLII _____

22. CMXCIX _____

Roman Rules Review

If you look back at the Roman numerals on the preceding pages, you will see that they followed these rules when writing numerals.

1. Don't use more than three symbols in a row.

wrong	right
VIIII = 9	IX = 9
XXXX = 40	XL = 40

2. Don't use more than one V, L, or D successively in a numeral.

wrong	right
VV = 10	X = 10
DD = 1000	M = 1,000

3. Do not **subtract** V, L, or D.

wrong	right
VL = 45	XLV = 45
LD = 450	CDL = 450

4. The **I** may only be subtracted from V and X. **X** may only be subtracted from L and C. **C** may only be subtracted from D and M. Generally, this means that the subtraction rule is only used to designate the numerals for 4, 9, 40, 90, 400, and 900.

wrong	right
IL = 49	XLIX = 49
XD = 490	CDXC = 490

Use the rules above to choose the right way to write each numeral below in Roman numerals. Circle the correct notation.

1.	19	XVIIII	XIX	IXX
2.	44	XXXXIV	XLIIII	XLIV
3.	95	LXXXXV	VC	XCV
4.	105	LXXXXVVV	CV	CIIIII
5.	49	XLIX	XXXXIX	XLVIIII
6.	75	LXXIIIII	LXXV	LXVVV
7.	449	CDXXXXIX	CCCCXLIX	CDXLIX
8.	495	VD	CDXCV	CDLXXXXV
9.	900	DCCCLL	CM	DCCCC

Writing Roman Numerals

Test your knowledge of Roman numerals by writing the numerals below in the Roman number system. Use the following symbols.

I = 1   V = 5   X = 10   L = 50

C = 100   D = 500   M = 1000

1. 14 _____

2. 27 _____

3. 39 _____

4. 53 _____

5. 74 _____

6. 48 _____

7. 112 _____

8. 159 _____

9. 95 _____

10. 243 _____

11. 364 _____

12. 206 _____

13. 197 _____

14. 515 _____

15. 750 _____

16. 400 _____

17. 475 _____

18. 654 _____

19. 1,111 _____

20. 2,500 _____

21. 2,356 _____

22. 1,740 _____

23. 930 _____

24. 3,224 _____

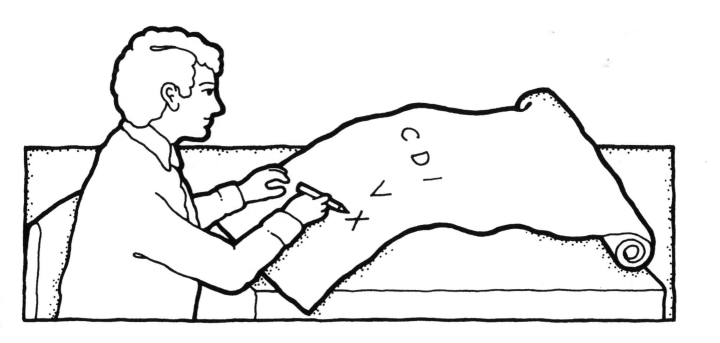

29

Even Larger Roman Numerals

Remember the Roman numeral system uses seven letters to denote numbers. These are:

I = 1	V = 5	X = 10	L = 50
C = 100	D = 500	M = 1000	

To write a numeral larger than MMMCMXCIX (3,999), you draw a bar over the numeral to represent thousands. A bar over a numeral means that number times 1,000.

$\overline{V}$ = 5,000 $\overline{X}$ = 10,000

$\overline{CV}$ = 105,000 $\overline{IX}$LII = 9,052

Read these Roman numerals and write them in our number system.

1. $\overline{L}$ _____

2. $\overline{D}$ _____

3. $\overline{XC}$ _____

4. $\overline{VCL}$ _____

5. $\overline{VIII}$XV _____

6. $\overline{CDCX}$ _____

7. $\overline{CCIX}$ _____

8. $\overline{CMDV}$ _____

9. $\overline{LXX}$CL _____

10. $\overline{DCCC}$LX _____

Write these numerals as Roman numerals.

11. 60,000 _____

12. 800,000 _____

13. 4,015 _____

14. 7,300 _____

15. 9,675 _____

16. 10,500 _____

17. 17,450 _____

18. 150,700 _____

19. 360,060 _____

20. 400,000 _____

Counting Like a Greek

Like the Roman number system, the Greek number system assigned numerical values to the letters of the alphabet. They used the 24 letters of the Greek alphabet plus three additional characters that are now obsolete to denote numbers. The first nine letters of their early alphabet represented the numerals one through nine. The next nine letters represented multiples of ten, from ten to ninety. The next nine letters represented multiples of one hundred, from one to nine hundred. At first capital letters were used. Later they used lower case letters. The Greek numerals up to 999 were quite easy to read, if you knew all the symbols. However, 27 symbols were a lot to remember.

A	alpha	1	I	iota	10	P	rho	100
B	beta	2	K	kappa	20	Σ	sigma	200
Γ	gamma	3	Λ	lambda	30	T	tau	300
Δ	delta	4	M	mu	40	Υ	upsilon	400
E	epsilon	5	N	nu	50	Φ	phi	500
Ϛ	digamma	6	Ξ	xi	60	X	chi	600
Z	zeta	7	O	omnicron	70	Ψ	psi	700
H	eta	8	Π	pi	80	Ω	omega	800
Θ	theta	9	Ϙ	koppa	90	ϡ	sampi	900

To write numerals, the Greek simply combined the symbols from the chart and added the values for each symbol. Here are some examples.

NB = 50 + 2 = 52

XΘ = 600 + 9 = 609

ΨIH = 700 + 10 + 8 = 718

ΣNΔ = 200 + 50 + 4 = 254

Read these Greek numerals and write their value in our number system.

1. Θ = _____

2. Λ = _____

3. Σ = _____

4. KΔ = _____

5. ΞH = _____

6. OΘ = _____

7. TI = _____

8. MΔ = _____

9. PNE = _____

10. ΨΛE = _____

11. TΠΔ = _____

12. ΥKA = _____

Writing Greek Numerals

Use the chart of Greek numerals to write the following as Greek numerals.

1. 830 = _____

2. 313 = _____

3. 222 = _____

4. 305 = _____

5. 404 = _____

6. 768 = _____

7. 81 = _____

8. 887 = _____

9. 555 = _____

10. 68 = _____

11. 777 = _____

12. 122 = _____

13. 639 = _____

14. 889 = _____

15. 551 = _____

One problem with the Greek's system was that some numerals also spelled words. This could sometimes be confusing. It also led to superstitions about numbers that people associated with initials or with words they spelled. As you will see with the next problems, it might be hard to tell if a Greek was writing a word or a numeral.

Write the following as Greek numerals.

16. 370 _____

17. 45 _____

18. 78 _____

19. 375 _____

20. 315 _____

21. 41 _____

Comparing Greek Numerals

Use >, < or = to compare the pairs of numerals below.

1. Θ _____ O

2. Z _____ I

3. M _____ N

4. M _____ K

5. OΔ _____ TH

6. X _____ Φ

7. Σ _____ Ω

8. ΦΞΒ _____ Ψ

9. ΠΖ _____ NH

10. TΘ _____ TΠ

11. TK _____ TIZ

12. N _____ ME

13. PA _____ XA

14. ΦOZ _____ ΥIB

15. Π _____ Λ

16. NZ _____ ΩZ

17. PΠH _____ PMΓ

18. ΥΞE _____ ΥKΔ

19. ΦΠΘ _____ X

20. ΦMΓ _____ Π

21. TA _____ TE

22. ΞΘ _____ OA

23. Φ _____ Ω

24. Ψ _____ XA

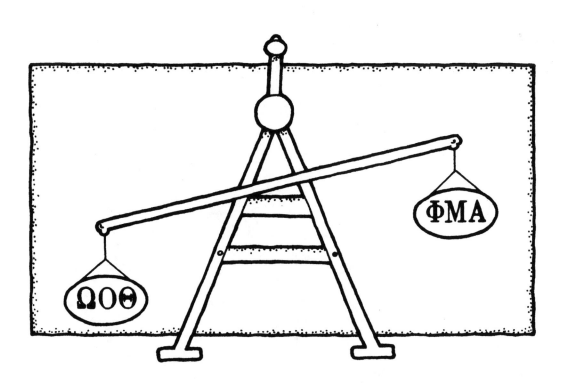

On Your Own with Greek Numerals

A	1	I	10	P	100
B	2	K	20	Σ	200
Γ	3	Λ	30	T	300
Δ	4	M	40	Υ	400
E	5	N	50	Φ	500
obsolete	6	Ξ	60	X	600
Z	7	O	70	Ψ	700
H	8	Π	80	Ω	800
Θ	9	obsolete	90	obsolete	900

Refer to the chart of Greek numerals and write the numerals below using the Greek number symbols.

1. 30 _____

2. 50 _____

3. 17 _____

4. 82 _____

5. 48 _____

6. 75 _____

7. 354 _____

8. 231 _____

9. 623 _____

10. 467 _____

11. 809 _____

12. 108 _____

13. 727 _____

14. 450 _____

15. 575 _____

16. 343 _____

17. 281 _____

18. 604 _____

19. 612 _____

20. 821 _____

21. 439 _____

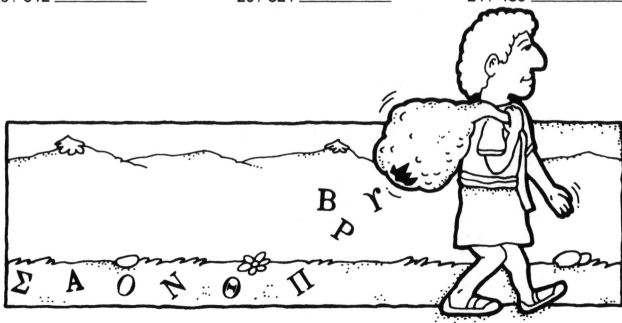

34

More Practice with Greek Numerals

Write the following Greek numerals in our decimal number system.

1. ΟΕ _____

2. ΩΠΗ _____

3. ΤΛ _____

4. ΛΖ _____

5. ΦΟ _____

6. ΤΜ _____

7. ΣΛΔ _____

8. ΡΔ _____

9. ΨΙΑ _____

10. ΦΚ _____

11. ΣΠΗ _____

12. ΨΝΑ _____

13. ΣΗ _____

14. ΤΟΒ _____

15. ΨΖ _____

16. ΧΠ _____

17. ΥΜΘ _____

18. ΤΚΘ _____

It may **seem** like the Greeks had place value, since they had symbols for *hundreds*, *tens*, and *ones*. However, it was the symbol that represented hundreds not its placement. For example, Σ = 200, whether it stood alone or with other symbols. You could write ΣΜ or ΜΣ, ΣΕ or ΕΣ. The placement of Σ in the numeral did not change its value. It was always equal to 200.

19. Write your age in Greek numerals. _____

20. What is the largest numeral you can write using the 24 Greek numerals? _____

    Write this numeral two other ways. _____

Writing Larger Greek Numerals

Using the 27 original letters of the ancient Greek alphabet the Greeks could write the numerals from 1 to 999. When the Greeks wanted to write numerals in the thousands they used the symbols from 1 to 9 followed by a "prime" sign ('). This meant that the number was multiplied by 1,000. For example;

A' = 1,000   B' = 2,000   Γ'ΝΖ = 3,057
  (1 x 1000)   (2 x 1000)   (3 x 1000) + 50 + 7

Refer to a chart of Greek numerals and write these Greek numerals in our number system.

1. Δ'_____   2. H'_____   3. E'ΧΓ _____

4. A'ΣΛ _____   5. Z'ΠΔ _____   6. Γ'ΦΠ _____

7. Z'ΡΜΖ _____   8. Θ'ΧΙΗ _____   9. B'Σ _____

For **ten thousands** Greeks used the capital **M** with other symbols. They wrote the **M** with another number symbol written above it. The number on top of the **M** told how many 10,000's. Using the **M** to multiply numbers by 10,000 yielded the following numerals.

A
M = 10,000

Δ
M = 40,000

Z
MT = 70,300

E
MZ' = 57,000

Write these Greek numerals in our number system.

  E
1. MT = _____

  B
2. M = _____

  H
3. MΔ'H = _____

  Γ
4. M = _____

  A
5. MA'A = _____

  Δ
6. ME'ΣIE = _____

  B
7. MΔ'Π = _____

  Γ
8. MΔ' = _____

  Z
9. MOZ = _____

Comparing Ancient Number Systems

Complete this chart to compare the systems of numeration of the Egyptians, Babylonians, Romans, and Greeks.

	24	77	305	671
Egyptian				
Babylonian				
Roman				
Greek				

Which of these systems is easiest to use and why?

_____

_____

_____

_____

_____

Hindu-Arabic Numerals

The Hindu-Arabic number system is named after the Hindus who invented the system and the Arabs who transmitted it to western Europe. Its earliest use was documented in 250 B.C. It was not until 800 A.D., however, that they began to use zero and the concept of place value. The number system was carried by traders to Europe and by the 12th century was widely used throughout the western world. The symbols that were used in this system looked different from the ones we use today. As the people of Europe used the Hindu way of writing numerals, they changed them. By 1500, the present symbols were standardized. The invention of **zero** made possible a number system that offered the greatest advantages in terms of simplicity, economical use of symbols, and ease of computation. This system and its ten symbols are used around the world today.

The Hindu-Arabic system is today called the **decimal system.** This is because it is a base ten system, and **deci** means ten. This system uses ten number symbols (0, 1, 2, 3, 4, 5, 6, 7, 8, and 9).

The Hindu-Arabic system is also a **place value** system and uses zero as a place holder. In a place value system we do not simply add the sum of the digits. Instead, each numeral has a different **value,** depending on its **place** in the numeral. In the decimal system each place has a value that is ten times larger than the place to its right. A place value chart would look like this.

100,000's	10,000's	1,000's	100's	10's	1's

For this system to work, the **zero** is necessary as a place holder. For example, in 20, **zero** means *no ones.* In 105, **zero** means *no tens.* And in 2,068, **zero** means *no hundreds.*

What does the 2 represent in the following numerals?

1. 25 _____

2. 1,234 _____

3. 2,076 _____

4. 28,009 _____

Interpreting the Decimal System

Tell the actual value the given symbol represents in each numeral below. The first one is done for you.

1. The numeral 4 represents __40__ in 347 and __4,000__ in 4,297.

2. The numeral 1 represents _____ in 6,142 and _____ in 21,456.

3. The numeral 6 represents _____ in 526 and _____ in 36,300.

4. The numeral 8 represents _____ in 1,845 and _____ in 4,583.

5. The numeral 2 represents _____ in 9,287 and _____ in 2,978.

6. The numeral 7 represents _____ in 75 and _____ in 75,000.

7. The numeral 3 represents _____ in 13 and _____ in 31,456.

8. The numeral 5 represents _____ in 57,432 and _____ in 57.

9. The numeral 9 represents _____ in 49 and _____ in 958,400.

Sometimes the same numeral is used more than once in a numeral. It represents different values according to its **places** in the numeral.

10. In 25,350 the 5 represents _____ and _____ .

11. In 72,745 the 7 represents _____ and _____ .

12. In 303,600 the 3 represents _____ and _____ .

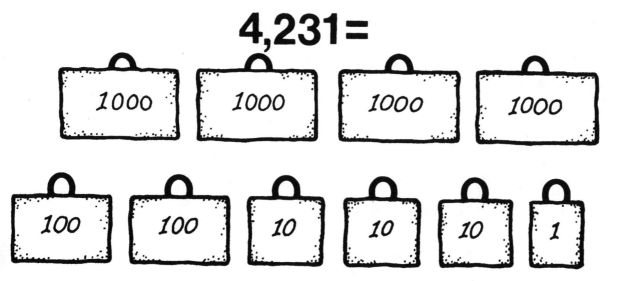

Understanding Place Value

The Hindu-Arabic number system is called the decimal system today because it is a base-ten place-value system. This means that the value of each symbol is determined by its placement, and each place is ten times greater than the place to the right. A place value table for the Hindu-Arabic system would look like the following. Fill in the missing parts.

billions			millions			hundreds	tens	ones
				10,000	1,000	100	10	1

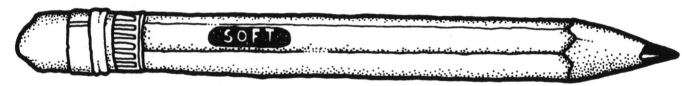

Write the following numerals in the decimal system.

1. Ten thousand, four hundred, thirty-six _____

2. Two hundred thousand, five hundred, fifty _____

3. Four hundred thousand, nineteen _____

4. Two million, three thousand, two hundred _____

5. Five million, one hundred thousand, ten _____

6. Ten million, twelve thousand, forty-five _____

7. One hundred million, five thousand, one hundred _____

8. Five hundred fifty million, five hundred thousand _____

9. Two billion, three hundred thousand _____

10. Five billion, five hundred million _____

11. Nine hundred ninety-nine million _____

12. Write the number that comes before one billion _____

The Quinary System

Fingers were a convenient counting device for people at all times in history. Several early number systems that were based on finger counting were extensively used. Since there are five fingers, these systems were base five systems. Germany used the base-five system on its calendars as late as 1800. Even today some South American tribes count by hands. They count by saying, "One, two, three, four, hand, hand plus one, hand plus two."

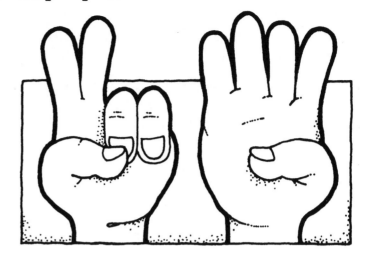

Quinary means five, so the quinary system is **based on five**. This number system uses **five** numerals (0, 1, 2, 3, and 4). If you were using these symbols to denote numbers using the ancient finger counting systems, 12 would mean one hand plus 2 fingers and would be read "one hand and two." In the quinary number system, we write 12_5 which is read "one-two base five" and means one five and two ones.

In the quinary system the value of each place is **five times** greater than the position to its right.

(5 x 25)	(5 x 5)	(5 x 1)	(1 x 1)
125	25	5	1

So in the quinary or base-five system, 10 is **not** ten; 10 is **five**. It represents $(1 \times 5) + (0 \times 1)$.

Here is how you would count to ten in the quinary system and how the quinary notation compares with the decimal notation.

Quinary	1	2	3	4	10	11	12	13	14	20
Decimal	1	2	3	4	5	6	7	8	9	10

Important Note: When reading base five numerals, read 20_5 as two-zero, not twenty. Remember that the 2 represents two 5's and the 0 represents zero ones.

---

1. What does 20 mean in base five? _____

2. What does 34 mean in base five? _____

3. What does 14 mean in base five? _____

4. What does 23 mean in base five? _____

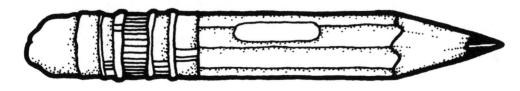

Base Five Place Value

Remember, in base five the first place on the right is **ones**. The value of each other place is **five times** the place to its right.

Interpret the numerals written in the place value chart below.

Base Five　　　　　　　　　　　　　　　　　　　　　　**Decimal**

	125's	25's	5's	1's	
1. 43_5			4	3	_____
2. 112_5		1	1	2	_____
3. 134_5		1	3	4	_____
4. 201_5		2	0	1	_____
5. 214_5		2	1	4	_____
6. 243_5		2	4	3	_____
7. 320_5		3	2	0	_____
8. 431_5		4	3	1	_____
9. 1010_5	1	0	1	0	_____
10. 1123_5	1	1	2	3	_____
11. 1142_5	1	1	4	2	_____
12. 2014_5	2	0	1	4	_____

Extending Understanding of the Quinary System

In the quinary system the value of each place is five times greater than the position to its right, so the value of the fifth place is 625 (or 5 x 125).

625's	125's	25's	5's	1's

The value of the next place to the left would be 5 x 625 or _____

100000_5 = _____ $_{10}$

Tell the **actual value in our number system** represented by the given numeral in the base-five numerals below. The first is done for you.

1. The numeral 2 represents __10__ in 20_5 and __250__ in 2110_5.

2. The numeral 1 represents _____ in 312_5 and _____ in 1203_5.

3. The numeral 3 represents _____ in 312_5 and _____ in 1312_5.

4. The numeral 4 represents _____ in 204_5 and _____ in 2400_5.

5. The numeral 1 represents _____ in 123_5 and _____ in 12300_5.

6. The numeral 2 represents _____ in 241_5 and _____ in 21430_5.

7. The numeral 3 represents _____ in 231_5 and _____ in 13420_5.

8. The numeral 4 represents _____ in 342_5 and _____ in 24300_5.

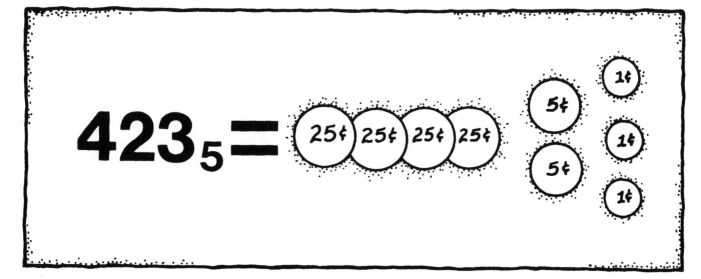

Interpreting Quinary Numerals

Once you understand the place value of the quinary number system you can become an expert "Q.D.I." (Quinary-Decimal Interpreter).

All the numerals on the left side of the charts below are written in the quinary (base-five) number system. Your challenge is to write the equivalent numeral in the decimal (base-ten) number system.

Quinary	Decimal
a. 34_5	
b. 100_5	
c. 123_5	
d. 144_5	
e. 212_5	
f. 231_5	
g. 304_5	
h. 320_5	
i. 343_5	

Quinary	Decimal
j. 1000_5	
k. 1020_5	
l. 1103_5	
m. 1142_5	
n. 1210_5	
o. 1244_5	
p. 1301_5	
q. 1330_5	
r. 1424_5	

Counting in the Quinary System

Fill in the missing numerals in the base five counting chart below.

1 __ __ __ __ 11 __ __ __ __ __ __ __ __ 24 __ __ __ __ __

40 __ __ __ __ __ 101 __ __ __ __ __ 112 __ __ __ __

__ 124 __ __ __ __ __ __ __ __ __ __ __ 200

Counting in the base five system, write the numeral that comes after each of the numerals given below.

a. 200_5 _____

b. 204_5 _____

c. 244_5 _____

d. 310_5 _____

e. 324_5 _____

f. 344_5 _____

g. 404_5 _____

h 434_5 _____

i. 440_5 _____

j. 444_5 _____

k. 1010_5 _____

l. 1044_5 _____

m. 1142_5 _____

n. 1233_5 _____

o. 1304_5 _____

p. 1344_5 _____

q. 1400_5 _____

r. 14044_5 _____

s. 1434_5 _____

t. 1444_5 _____

134   3131   11
14   1323
324   44
1034

Counting Like a Computer

The **decimal** system is based on **ten** and uses ten number symbols. The **quinary** system is based on **five** and uses five symbols. **Bi** means two. So you can probably guess that the **binary system** is based on **two** and uses only two numerals (0 and 1). The binary number system is used today primarily to program computers.

The binary system's place value works just like that of the decimal and quinary system, except that it is based on powers of **two**. The first place on the right is ones. The value of each place to the left is two times greater than the position to its right. The place values of numerals written in this system are as follows.

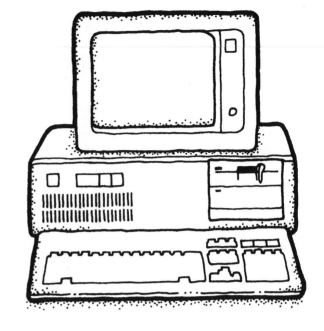

(2x8)	(2x4)	(2x2)	(2x1)	(1x1)
16	8	4	2	1

This means that $110_2 = (1\times4) + (1\times2) + (0\times1) = 6_{10}$

Another example is $1001_2 = (1\times8) + (0\times4) + (0\times2) + (1\times1) = 9_{10}$

Here is how you would count to ten in the binary or base two system.

Binary -	1	10	11	100	101	110	111	1000	1001	1010
Decimal -	1	2	3	4	5	6	7	8	9	10

Important Note: When reading binary numerals read 100_2 as "one-zero-zero" not "one hundred." Remember, the 1 represents one four and the 0's represent zero twos and zero ones.

Write the following as base two numerals.

1. Your age = _____ $_2$

2. Number of eggs in a carton = _____ $_2$

3. Number of senses humans have = _____ $_2$

4. Number of legs on your table and chair = _____ $_2$

5. Number of different things in your lunch today = _____ $_2$

Place Value – Base Two

Remember that in the binary system the first place on the right is **ones**. The value of each other place is **two times** the place to its right.

Interpret the binary numerals written in the place value chart below and write them as decimal numerals.

	16's	8's	4's	2's	1's	Decimal Numerals
a. 110_2			1	1	0 =	_____
b. 1101_2		1	1	0	1 =	_____
c. 1010_2		1	0	1	0 =	_____
d. 1111_2		1	1	1	1 =	_____
e. 10000_2	1	0	0	0	0 =	_____
f. 10101_2	1	0	1	0	1 =	_____
g. 11000_2	1	1	0	0	0 =	_____
h. 11011_2	1	1	0	1	1 =	_____
i. 10010_2	1	0	0	1	0 =	_____
j. 10110_2	1	0	1	1	0 =	_____
k. 11100_2	1	1	1	0	0 =	_____
l. 11101_2	1	1	1	0	1 =	_____
m. 11111_2	1	1	1	1	1 =	_____

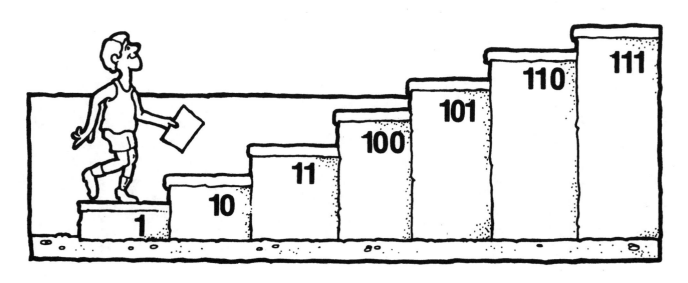

Binary Place Value Chart

Using only the number symbols "1" and "0" write each decimal numeral as a binary numeral by filling out the binary place value chart and then writing the numeral in base two.

Decimal Numerals	16's	8's	4's	2's	1's	Binary Numerals
a. 7_{10} =						
b. 12_{10} =						
c. 14_{10} =						
d. 20_{10} =						
e. 25_{10} =						
f. 18_{10} =						
g. 30_{10} =						
h. 23_{10} =						
i. 10_{10} =						
j. 17_{10} =						
k. 27_{10} =						
l. 11_{10} =						
m. 31_{10} =						

Larger Binary Numerals

Fill in the base-two place value chart below. Remember, the value of each place is **two times** the place to its right.

128's					4's	2's	1's

Now use your chart to help you interpret the binary numerals below.

Binary   Decimal   Binary   Decimal

a. 1110_2 = _____

b. 10111_2 = _____

c. 100101_2 = _____

d. 101000_2 = _____

e. 1000110_2 = _____

f. 1001001_2 = _____

g. 1100010_2 = _____

h. 11010_2 = _____

i. 10000010_2 = _____

j. 101101_2 = _____

k. 110010_2 = _____

l. 1011000_2 = _____

m. 10001001_2 = _____

n. 10000111_2 = _____

o. 10100010_2 = _____

p. 1011110_2 = _____

Comparing Decimal, Quinary and Binary Numerals

Complete this chart to compare decimal, quinary and binary systems of numeration.

Decimal	Quinary	Binary
5		
	14	
		1100
		11000
	210	
96		
		111111
	400	
		10001000

Mayan Number System

The Mayans lived in Central America from about 1500 B.C. to 1500 A.D. They developed a civilization that achieved great intellectual and artistic levels long before Columbus landed on the American continent. They had, in particular, remarkable knowledge in the areas of mathematics, astronomy, and chronology. At some point after 900 A.D. they mysteriously stopped working on their cities and religious centers and moved away from the cities. Historians do not know why they abandoned their ceremonial centers, but by the time the Spanish arrived in the 16th century, the Mayan civilization had been dead for several generations and their cities had fallen into ruin.

Cut off from other civilizations, the Mayans developed their own unique numeration system. Their system was a place-value system that had a symbol for zero. They used dots and bars as tally marks. One dot stood for 1, two dots stood for 2, three dots stood for 3, and four dots stood for 4. A horizontal bar stood for 5.

● = 1   ●● = 2   ●●● = 3   ●●●● = 4   ——— = 5

The Mayans used combinations of dots and bars to write the numerals 1 to 19.

● / ——— = 6   ●● / ——— = 7   ●●● / ——— = 8

●●●● / ——— = 9   === = 10   ● / === = 11

●● / === = 12   ●●● / === = 13   ●●●● / === = 14

≡ = 15   ● / ≡ = 16   ●● / ≡ = 17

●●● / ≣ = 18   ●●●● / ≣ = 19

The Mayan symbol for zero looked like this ⊖ It is believed to represent a clam shell.

Writing Mayan Numerals

Remember that the Mayans used a number system that used a ● to represent one and ── to represent five. They used a symbol that looked like ⊖ to represent zero. By combining these symbols, they could write numerals from zero to nineteen.

Write the answers to the following questions using Mayan numerals.

1. Count from zero to eighteen by two's (even numbers) using Mayan number symbols.

2. Count from zero to eighteen by three's using Mayan number symbols.

3. Write Mayan numerals to represent the following things:

   - The number of pets you have

   - How old you are when you can get a driver's license

   - How many jeans you own

   - How many pencils in your desk

   - The month you were born

Mayan Place Value

In the Mayan system place value was indicated by writing one symbol **above** another symbol, rather than horizontally. The Mayan system was based on **twenty**. Therefore, multiples of twenty were indicated by writing a symbol in a different place (above the other symbols). The place value was used to write numerals greater than nineteen. To write the numeral **20** the Mayans wrote their symbol for zero in the bottom row, and one dot in the second row.
It looked like this. ⬤ = 20

To write numerals larger than twenty, the bottom row represented **ones** and the second row represented **twenties**. Both were indicated by the dot symbol. For example:

⬤⬤ = 2   ⬤ over ⬤ = (1x20) + (1x1) = 21   ⬤⬤ over ⬤⬤⬤⬤ = (2x20) + (4x1) = 44

Notice that the numerals for **six** and **twenty-five** look very much alike. The difference is that in the "6" the dot is close to the bar. In the "25" there is more space between the dot and the bar.

⎯•⎯ = 6   ⎯•⎯ = 25

Interpret these Mayan numerals.

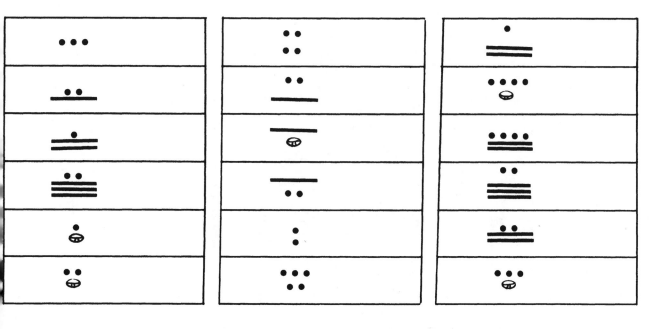

Counting Like a Mayan

In this exercise you will be reading Mayan numerals and writing them as decimal numerals. Remember the following things about the Mayan number system.

1. ● = 1 and ⎯ = 5.
2. ⊖ = 0 and was used as a placeholder.
3. It was a base-20 place value system.
4. Place value was indicated vertically by writing ●'s and ⎯'s above other symbols.

a. ●●●● ⎯	b. ●●●● ⎯ ●●	c. ⎯⎯⎯
d. ● ⎯	e. ⎯ ⊖	f. ●● ⊖
g. ● ⎯⎯⎯	h. ●● ⎯ ●●	i. ●● ⎯ ●
j. ● ●●● ⎯	k. ⎯ ●●● ⎯	l. ●● ⎯⎯
m. ●●● ⎯	n. ⎯⎯ ●●●●	o. ●●● ● ⎯
p. ●● ●●●●	q. ⎯⎯⎯ ⊖	r. ⎯ ●

Writing Mayan Numerals

Write the numerals below in the Mayan system. Remember spacing is important to distinguish between some numerals. For instance,

_____•_____ 6 and _____•_____ 25 look very similar except for the spacing.

a. 8 =	g. 41 =	m. 70 =	s. 104 =
b. 17=	h. 48 =	n. 77 =	t. 108 =
c. 20 =	i. 50 =	o. 85 =	u. 115 =
d. 25 =	j. 56 =	p. 92	v. 120 =
e. 30 =	k. 60 =	q. 99 =	w. 162 =
f. 37 =	l. 63 =	r. 100 =	x. 200 =

Larger Mayan Numerals

Since the Mayan number system was based on **twenty**, the first place (bottom) represented **ones**, and second place represented twenty times one, or **20**. The third place should have represented 20 x 20 or **400**, but it didn't. At this point, they switched to 360, because this was close to the number of lunar days in a year and fit in with their religious beliefs. A chart showing vertical place value of their numerals would look like this.

360's   (20x18)
20's   (20x1)
1's   (1x1)

The Mayans would write 400 in this way.

•   1 x 360
••   2 x 20
⊖   0 x 1

Here are some other examples.

= 361   = 403   = 725

Write the decimal equivalents of these Mayan numerals.

a.	b.	c.
d.	e.	f.
g.	h.	i.
j.	k.	l.
m.	n.	o.

Writing Larger Mayan Numerals

Write the numerals below in the Mayan number system. Remember, Mayan place value is based on **twenty** and places are **vertical**. Spacing of the dots and bars is important.

Examples

1167_{10}

• • •   (3 x 360)

• • • •   (4x20)

<u>• •</u>   (7x1)

762_{10}

• •   (2x360)

• •   (2x20)

• •   (2x1)

a. 520 =	b. 1111	c. 888
d. 1444 =	e. 1036	f. 999
g. 1705 =	h. 1266	i. 2074
j. 3100 =	k. 3436	l. 4000

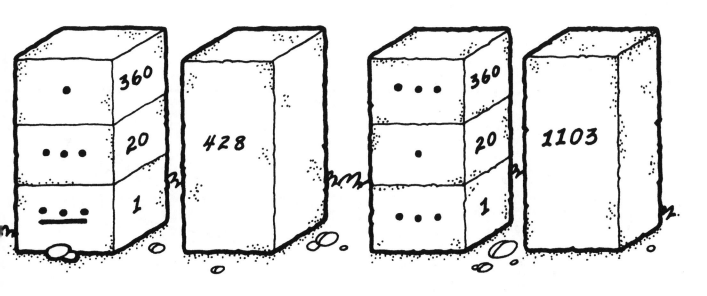

Review of all Ancient Number Systems

Complete this chart to compare the systems of numeration you have studied.

Write numerals for	14	47	304	1,568
Egyptian				
Babylonian				
Roman				
Greek				
Mayan				

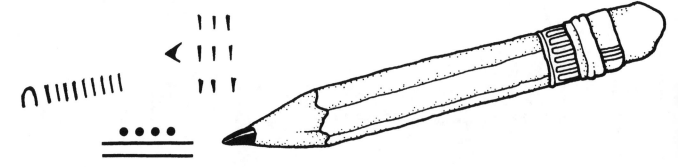

Answers

Primitive Number Symbols, p. 12
26, 33
Answers will vary

Egyptian Number System, p. 13
47 – 11 symbols   248 – 14 symbols
672 – 15 symbols   5,309 – 17 symbols

Count Like an Egyptian, p. 14
1. 143   2. 420
3. 2,605   4. 741
5. 37   6. 3,412
7. 1,600   8. 209
9. 662   10. 4,124
11. 3,306   12. 1,450
13. 6,162   14. 3,050
15. 542   16. 4,024
17. 2,305

Write Like an Egyptian, p. 15
1. 7 arches, 3 staffs
2. 1 coil, 3 arches, 9 staffs
3. 4 coils, 7 arches
4. 6 coils, 2 staffs
5. 3 flowers, 4 coils, 7 arches, 1 staff
6. 1 flower, 9 arches, 4 staffs
7. 2 flowers, 5 coils, 6 staffs
8. >   9. <
10. =   11. >
12. >

Larger Egyptian Numerals, p. 16
1. 5 fingers
2. 6 tadpoles
3. 2 men
4. 3 tadpoles, 2 fingers
5. 2 tadpoles, 5 fingers
6. 1 man, 4 tadpoles
7. 1 man, 7 fingers
8. 2 men, 2 tadpoles
25
54
999,999

Egyptian Review, p. 17
1. 30,132   2. 1,022,310
3. 423,062   4. 52,104
5. 104,045   6. 2,313,330
7. 250,300   8. 81,136
9. 2 fingers, 4 flowers, 6 coils, 1 arch, 2 staffs
10. 1 tadpole, 2 fingers, 5 coils, 3 arches, 4 staffs
11. 1 man, 4 fingers, 2 flowers, 1 arch, 5 staffs
12. 4 men, 1 finger, 3 coils, 7 arches, 8 staffs
13. 4 fingers, 4 flowers, 3 arches, 5 staffs
14. 3 tadpoles, 1 finger, 4 flowers, 2 coils, 7 arches, 5 staffs

Egyptian Computation, p. 18
1. 6 coils, 1 arch, 1 staff
2. 2 coils, 1 arch, 8 staffs
3. 6 coils, 2 arches, 2 staffs
4. 9 arches, 2 staffs
5. 1 flower, 6 arches, 2 staffs
6. 1 coil, 9 arches, 7 staffs
7. 5 coils, 6 staffs
8. 2 coils, 7 arches, 6 staffs

Reading and Writing Babylonian Numerals, p. 20
1. 36   2. 55
3. 21   4. 44
5. 33   6. 14
7. 42   8. 39

9.   10.

11.   12.

13.   14.

A Bright Babylonian Idea, p. 21
a. 78   b. 164
c. 81   d. 194
e. 339   f. 66

Reading Larger Babylonian Numerals, p. 22

1. 44	2. 163
3. 190	4. 89
5. 34	6. 319
7. 366	8. 142
9. 247	10. 283

Babylonian Review, p. 23

g. 49	h. 96
i. 348	j. 122

Even Larger Babylonian Numerals, p. 24

a. 797	b. 555
c. 907	d. 1,342
e. 2,000	f. 1,506

Roman Number System, p. 25

a. 6	b. 4
c. 11	d. 9
e. 16	f. 34
g. 33	h. 19

More Roman Numerals, p. 26

1. 62	2. 75	3. 59
4. 48	5. 150	6. 171
7. 164	8. 139	9. 141
10. 109	11. 106	12. 49
13. 90	14. 255	15. 330
16. 177	17. 144	18. 219
19. 195	20. 88	21. 243
22. 364	23. 296	24. 244

Larger Roman Numerals, p. 27

1. 600	12. 655
2. 1500	13. 1800
3. 740	14. 810
4. 1,224	15. 1,555
5. 439	16. 1,405
6. 2,310	17. 3,040
7. 975	18. 440
8. 1,412	19. 1,776
9. 944	20. 3,609
10. 1,900	21. 2,952
11. 1,492	22. 999

Roman Rules Review, p. 28

1. XIX	2. XLIV
3. XCV	4. CV
5. XLIX	6. LXXV
7. CDXLIX	8. CDXCV
9. CM	

Writing Roman Numerals, p. 29

1. XIV	2. XXVII
3. XXXIX	4. LIII
5. LXXIV	6. XLVIII
7. CXII	8. CLIX
9. XCV	10. CCXLIII
11. CCCLXIV	12. CCVI
13. CXCVII	14. DXV
15. DCCL	16. CD
17. CDLXXV	18. DCLIV
19. MCXI	20. MMD
21. MMCCCLVI	22. MDCCXL
23. CMXXX	24. MMMCCXXIV

Even Larger Roman Numerals, p. 30

1. 50,000	11. $\overline{LX}$
2. 500,000	12. $\overline{DCCC}$
3. 90,000	13. $\overline{IV}XV$
4. 5,150	14. $\overline{VII}CCC$
5. 8,015	15. $\overline{IX}DCLXXV$
6. 100,610	16. $\overline{XD}$
7. 200,009	17. $\overline{XVII}CDL$
8. 900,505	18. $\overline{CLD}CC$
9. 70,150	19. $\overline{CCCLX}LX$
10. 800,060	20. $\overline{CD}$

Counting Like a Greek, p. 31

1. 9	5. 68	9. 155
2. 30	6. 79	10. 735
3. 200	7. 310	11. 384
4. 24	8. 44	12. 421

Writing Greek Numerals, p. 32

1. ΩΛ	2. ΤΙΓ	3. ΣΚΒ
4. ΤΕ	5. ΥΔ	6. ΨΞΗ
7. ΠΑ	8. ΩΠΖ	9. ΦΝΕ
10. ΞΗ	11. ΨΟΖ	12. ΡΚΒ
13. ΧΛΘ	14. ΩΠΘ	15. ΦΝΑ
16. ΤΟ	17. ΜΕ	18. ΟΗ
19. ΤΟΕ	20. ΤΙΕ	21. ΜΑ

Comparing Greek Numerals, p. 33

1. <	9. >	17. >
2. <	10. <	18. >
3. <	11. >	19. <
4. >	12. >	20. >
5. <	13. <	21. <
6. >	14. >	22. <
7. <	15. >	23. <
8. <	16. <	24. >

On Your Own With Greek Numerals, p. 34

1. Λ	2. Ν	3. ΙΖ
4. ΠΒ	5. ΜΗ	6. ΟΕ
7. ΤΝΔ	8. ΣΛΑ	9. ΧΚΓ
10. ΥΞΖ	11. ΩΘ	12. ΡΗ
13. ΨΚΖ	14. ΥΝ	15. ΦΟΕ
16. ΤΜΓ	17. ΣΠΑ	18. ΧΔ
19. ΧΙΒ	20. ΩΚΑ	21. ΥΛΘ

More Practice with Greek Numerals, p. 35

1. 75	2. 888	3. 330
4. 37	5. 570	6. 340
7. 234	8. 104	9. 711
10. 520	11. 288	12. 751
13. 208	14. 472	15. 707
16. 680	17. 449	18. 329

19. answers will vary
20. ΩΠΘ, any order using these three symbols

Writing Larger Greek Numerals, p. 36

1. 4,000	2. 8,000	3. 5,603
4. 1,230	5. 7,084	6. 3,580
7. 7,147	8. 9,618	9. 2,200

1. 50,300	2. 20,000	3. 84,008
4. 30,000	5. 11,001	6. 45,215
7. 24,080	8. 34,000	9. 70,077

Comparing Ancient Number Systems, p. 37

Egyptian

24 = 2 arches, 4 staffs
77 = 7 arches, 7 staffs
305 = 3 coils, 5 staffs
671 = 6 coils, 7 arches, 1 staff

Babylonian

Roman

24 = XXIV	77 = LXXVII
305 = CCCV	671 = DCLXXI

Greek

24 = ΚΔ	77 = ΟΖ
305 = ΤΕ	671 = ΧΟΑ

Hindu–Arabic Numerals, p. 38

1. 2 tens
2. 2 hundreds
3. 2 thousands
4. 2 ten thousands

Interpreting the Decimal System, p. 39

2. 100 and 1,000
3. 6 and 6,000
4. 800 and 80
5. 200 and 2,000
6. 70 and 70,000
7. 3 and 30,000
8. 50,000 and 50
9. 9 and 900,000
10. 5,000 and 50
11. 70,000 and 700
12. 300,000 and 3,000

Understanding Place Value, p. 40

billion	1,000,000,000
hundred million	100,000,000
ten million	10,000,000
million	1,000,000
hundred thousand	100,000
ten thousand	10,000
thousand	1,000
hundred	100
ten	10
one	1

Understanding Place Value, p. 40

1. 10,436	2. 200,550
3. 400,019	4. 2,003,200
5. 5,100,010	6. 10,012,045
7. 100,005,100	8. 550,500,000
9. 2,000,300,000	10. 5,500,000,000
11. 999,000,000	12. 999,999,999

The Quinary System, p. 41

1. 2 fives
2. 3 fives and 4 ones
3. 1 five and 4 ones
4. 2 fives and 3 ones

Base Five Place Value, p. 42

1. 23	2. 32
3. 44	4. 51
5. 59	6. 73
7. 85	8. 116
9. 130	10. 163
11. 172	12. 259

Extending Understanding of the Quinary System, p. 43

3. 125 and 3,125

2. 5 and 125	3. 75 and 75
4. 4 and 100	5. 25 and 625
6. 50 and 1250	7. 15 and 375
8. 20 and 500	

Interpreting Quinary Numerals, p. 44

a. 19	j. 125
b. 25	k. 135
c. 38	l. 153
d. 49	m. 172
e. 57	n. 180
f. 66	o. 199
g. 79	p. 201
h. 85	q. 215
i. 98	r. 239

Counting in the Quinary System, p. 45

1, 2, 3, 4, 10, 11, 12, 13, 14, 20, 21, 22, 23, 24, 30, 31, 32, 33, 34, 40, 41, 42, 43, 44, 100, 101, 102, 103, 104, 110, 111, 112, 113, 114, 120, 121, 122, 123, 124, 130, 131, 132, 133, 134, 140, 141, 142, 143, 144, 200

a. 201	k. 1011
b. 210	l. 1100
c. 300	m. 1143
d. 311	n. 1234
e. 330	o. 1310
f. 400	p. 1400
g. 410	q. 1401
h. 440	r. 14100
i. 441	s. 1440
j. 1000	t. 2000

Counting Like a Computer, p. 46

1. answers will vary   2. 1100
3. 101   4. 1000
5. answers will vary

Place Value – Base Two, p. 47

a. 6	h. 27
b. 13	i. 18
c. 10	j. 22
d. 15	k. 28
e. 16	l. 29
f. 21	m. 31
g. 24	

Binary Place Value Chart, p. 48

a. 111	h. 10111
b. 1100	i. 1010
c. 1110	j. 10001
d. 10100	k. 11011
e. 11001	l. 1011
f. 10010	m. 11111
g. 11110	

Larger Binary Numerals, p. 49

a. 14	i. 130
b. 23	j. 45
c. 37	k. 50
d. 40	l. 88
e. 70	m. 137
f. 73	n. 135
g. 98	o. 162
h. 26	p. 94

Comparing Decimal, Quinary and Binary Numerals, p. 50

Decimal	Quinary	Binary
5	10	**101**
9	14	1001
12	22	1100
24	44	11000
55	210	110111
96	341	1100000
63	223	111111
100	400	1100100
136	**1021**	10001000

Writing Mayan Numerals, p. 52

1. see proper notation on preceding page
2. see proper notation of preceding page
3. answers will vary

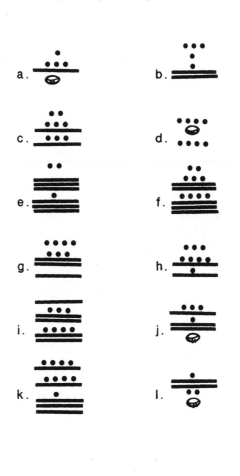

Egyptian
14 = 1 arch, 4 staffs
47 = 4 arches, 7 staffs
304 = 3 coils, 4 staffs
1568 = 1 flower, 5 coils, 6 arches, 8 staffs

Babylonian

Roman
14 = XIV   47 = XLVII
304 = CCCIV   1568 = MDLXVIII

Greek
14 = IΔ   47 = MZ
304 = TΔ

1568 = A'ΦΞH

Mayan

64

Can You Count In Greek?

All lessons in this book align to the following standards.

Grade Level	Common Core State Standards in Math
Grade 3	3.OA.A Represent and solve problems involving multiplication and division. 3.OA.C Multiply and divide within 100. 3.OA.D Solve problems involving the four operations, and identify and explain patterns in arithmetic. 3.NBT.A Use place value understanding and properties of operations to perform multi-digit arithmetic.
Grade 4	4.OA.A Use the four operations with whole numbers to solve problems. 4.OA.C Generate and analyze patterns. 4.NBT.A Generalize place value understanding for multi-digit whole numbers. 4.NBT.B Use place value understanding and properties of operations to perform multi-digit arithmetic.
Grade 5	5.OA.A Write and interpret numerical expressions. 5.OA.B Analyze patterns and relationships. 5.NBT.A Understand the place value system.
Grade 6	6.EE.A Apply and extend previous understandings of arithmetic to algebraic expressions. 6.EE.B Reason about and solve one-variable equations and inequalities.

Key: OA = Operations & Algebraic Thinking; NBT = Number & Operations in Base Ten; EE = Expressions & Equations

Printed in the United States
by Baker & Taylor Publisher Services